Super Big Brother
and
Sweet Little Sister

BY TOLU ADEOSUN (MAMA TEE)

Balboa Press books may be ordered through booksellers or by contacting:

Balboa Press
A Division of Hay House
1663 Liberty Drive
Bloomington, IN 47403
www.balboapress.com
844-682-1282

ISBN: 978-1-9822-6078-1 (sc)
ISBN: 978-1-9822-6077-4 (e)

Print information available on the last page.

Balboa Press rev. date: 12/30/2020

BALBOA.PRESS
A DIVISION OF HAY HOUSE

Super Big Brother
and
Sweet Little Sister

This book is dedicated to my sweethearts: Ayobami, Ayodeji, and Tiwalayo. You all inspire me.

Super Big Brother

Hi, my name is Tiwa and I am a brand new baby

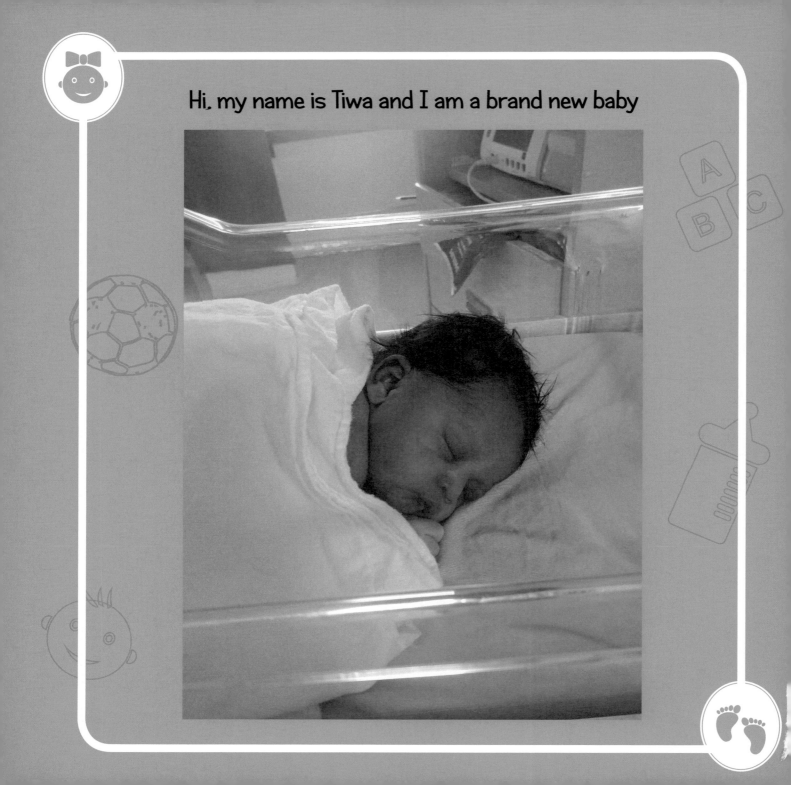

I have a big brother who is pretty super.

His name is Deji, he is 3 and a half year old.

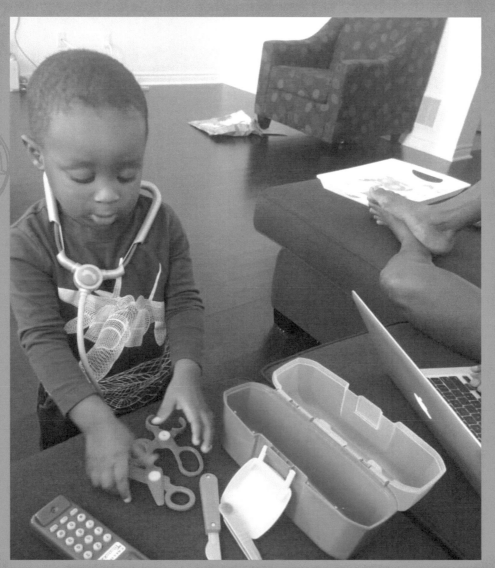

He is my superhero, and I'm pretty sure my mom's too.

He is always ready to help our mom.
When I need a bottle, he helps to feed me. When I need a diaper change, he brings mommy my diapers.
When I need to be held, he offers to hold me.

My super big brother doesn't like to see me cry

He always sings to me and rocks me as well.

My super big brother tells me I am here
My super big brother says I love you baby sister
And I love him too.

Sweet Little Sister

Hi, my name is Deji I am almost four years old. I'm going to be a big brother

I asked my mother for a baby brother or sister in January 2018. My mom said why don't you pray for one? I took my mom seriously and I started to pray for a sibling.

One day my mommy told me that I am going to be a big brother. I was super excited! Finally God heard my prayers.

My mom would show me pictures of the baby every time she went for an appointment where they take pictures of the baby inside of her tummy. Mommy says it's called an ultrasound.

Every time mommy would show me the picture of my baby brother or baby sister. I would always guess it was a sweet little sister.

One day in October, mommy revealed to me that I was going to have a sweet little sister.

I was so excited because I was right ! I couldn't wait to meet my new baby sister.

On Feb 25, 2019 mommy and daddy went to the hospital to have my sister. I got to stay with grandma, she is lots of fun and filled with love.

I then got to meet my sweet little sister at the hospital.

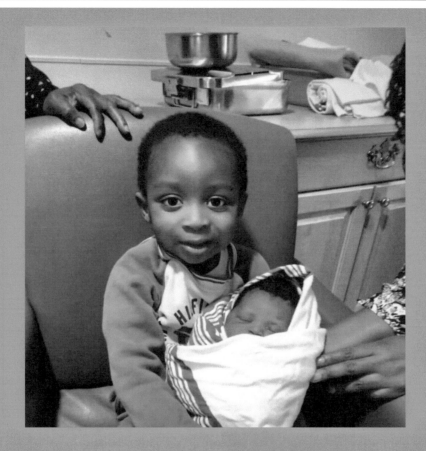

She was so beautiful and so tiny, I wasn't allowed to hold her by myself. I told my sweet little sister that I am here and that I love her.

I had to leave the hospital and go back home. My sweet little sister came home a few days later. I had this feeling that she was sick. I started to sing and pray for her to get better.

My mom said she had jaundice, it's a condition that makes babies of all different kinds of color turn yellow. This happens to some babies when they are born. Mommy said that I had the same condition when I was born and that we both had to stay longer in the hospital for light therapy.

I was happy that my sweet little sister was doing better. Everywhere I would go I would introduce myself as brother! My mother calls me super big brother because I like to take care of my sister. Oh did I tell you what my sister did when she came home from the hospital? She brought me lots of new toys! Isn't she a sweet little sister?

Printed in the United States
By Bookmasters